Dedicated to my Mother Heidi, without you none of this would have been possible.

Thank you to Han and Liam for your unwavering love, support, and belief in me.

Thank you Megan for your loyalty and friendship during the hardships I've endured.

And of course to Koda. I hope this inspires you to always speak your truth, set boundaries, and follow your heart.

I love you all.

The Storm

Chapter 1

All creation comes from a vortex. However, each vortex varies. The works before you were born from a vortex of pain so deep sometimes I could hardly perceive the light of day. I release these works to you in hopes that you can find some of yourself in these pages. The collective consciousness is awakening and part of awakening is pain. It is my hope that my words will ignite your soul, helping you to face yourself and what you have endured.

A Dime a Dozen

the narcissist will
claim
himself muse
behind the works
bore from the depths
of women's constant strife

placing himself on a pedestal
when really...
he is the pebble beneath our collective heel

because encountering a narcissist is so
common
it has become part
of a woman's walk of life

A True Pyramid Scheme

every time
I build a pyramid
with a man
I will always
be at the bottom

my bones a part
of the foundation

while he erects
a monument to
himself
on my grave

As Above So Below

a concept uttered repetitively in spiritual context
a vague illusion I had a loose grasp on

never fully understood
then I realized...

nature illustrates truth for us
plain as day

what is the surface of a crystal clear lake if not a projection?
so too, is our own power revealed to us

we do not just come from Mother Earth
we are her children

what she projects -
trees,
mountains,
rain,
clouds,
storms,
sun,
calm
all that she is, reflected back at her

as above so below

our own terrain,
storm,
foliage,
beauty,
chaos,
tranquility
are mirrored back to us
we too project
a gateway into our own realities
as above so below

Authenticity

when did we start
equating emotion
with weakness?

when the ego
took over the
role of the soul

the ego is like a helmet
meant to preserve
the face and
shield the mind

but when you
bare your soul
it takes true
courage

to crack open your chest
and put your suffering
on display for
the world to see

so the next time
someone calls you
sensitive
as an insult
say
"thank you"

because you are a medical miracle
walking around
with your heart
on your sleeve

Avalanche

it won't be
one colossal choice
that destroys you
rather it will be
the collective small choices
that snowball together
gaining speed and momentum
until finally
you'll find yourself
victim of a silent avalanche
caught unaware
struggling to breathe
stifled
silenced

people will talk to you
about faith
as they walk atop
the snow banks
that are crushing you

all of this
because you were
afraid
to be
alone
and now look
where you ended up
trapped
between each
collective choice
that led you
here

in isolation, you turn
inward
you chip away
at the ice inside your chest
berating yourself
but force only
strengthens the wall of ice
and so
you start to
feel

first anger radiates from your core
then as the ice starts to thaw
from the heat of your rage
naturally waves of sorrow wash over you
you find yourself treading
no longer contained
but still straining

as the storm starts to pass
your ability to recognize beauty returns
and suddenly
you find yourself
adrift on an island

still isolated
in a sense
but now you can
breathe
and
dream

Combustion

maybe the big bang
was simply God's
heart exploding

because I've noticed
all my best
creations
are propelled
by the
combustion
of each
heartache
I've endured

Dream

they say
"you can do
anything
you've ever
dreamed of"

the issue is a
nightmare
is also a
dream

Dualities

in a world of
dualities
why are we so
repulsed
by mental illness?

to me
at times
it seems almost a
natural reaction
to such a
heinously controlling society

two sides of one coin

capitalism and the
destruction it reigns down
upon humanity
encompassing
almost every aspect
of life
with it's evil tendrils

yet
flip the coin
and you'll find
humanity's persistence
in pursuing
good
truth
justice
love
friendship
equality
warmth
kindness

perhaps
these extreme
highs and lows are
natural

and sane people
are simply reacting
to an inhumane
society

Fragile

I know I'm too
fragile
for this love

because I find
the eggshells
I'm walking on
are my own

Fuck Boi

"make your own
happiness"
he said to me

but what he
didn't understand
was that I didn't
expect him to
lift me up

only
not to drag
me down to
hell

Full Circle

one defining moment

a window
where you peek back

you nod
"ah yes
that was it"

the moment
you let a man
(who was not even
a main character
in the movie of your life)
dictate your fate

innocently enough
it starts
he wanders over
to ask
"what do you plan for your
future?"

you reply
"write"

a shadow falls
he scoffs
laughs condescendingly
"ah, a writer"
he sneers

you feel a switch flip
in your heart
and now
you wonder
when before
you never guessed
that it wasn't enough

he walks away
you never see him again

but his words
are a fork in the road
and you leave your destiny
behind

luckily enough
life has a way of circling back

and now
armed with
experience
elation
devastation
death
torture
trauma
intimacy
and
insight

your pen sharper
than his opinion

Half Life

maybe
when you feel like
you want to die
when the torture is too
intense
it is because
part of you is dying

transforming can feel like
your soul is being
raked across torrid coals
agonizing
snaring every snag along the way
smiling faces gleam down on you
while your chest is ablaze

when you watch the phoenix fall
it appears to succumb
momentarily
then...
rebirth

no one tells you
how harrowing it is
to carry the ashes
of what once was
around in your chest
waiting for the next step
renewed life

but when it comes...
you will feel lighter than ever
before
wings will replace the ash
and you will discover
new heights

Illusion

seam: the stitching used to hold
two pieces of cloth together.

seem: an illusion that holds the
fabric of reality together.

to say that you
seem
to love me
I must decipher
whether or not
your love is
the thread holding us
together
or the illusion tearing me
apart

Imposter

fuck you to the
imposter
who proclaimed
"I would die for you"
but ran away
instead of offering a hand
when I was clinging onto
the ledge for dear life

as you walked
away
I did die
hand slipping off the
edge

May 2017

falling into the dark
abyss
which turned out to be
the dark night of the soul

yet despite everything
here I am
now
inhabiting another
peak
which you never
set foot on

Intuition

your intuition is the
fire in your belly

the narcissist is a
vacuum

as he gets closer and closer
the room is slowly
sapped
of oxygen
and suddenly your fire is
extinguished

without your internal
heat you are
a moth to a flame
flocking to the nearest light

unaware you are
headed straight towards
your own
destruction

Love Between

love between
a man and a woman
is reflected to us through
the relationship between
Mother Earth
and mankind

a man will praise
all a woman has to offer
using her resources
for his own devices
until she is
spent

a hollow shell
of her former
goddess

the shell will start to
crack
and blazing anger
will seep out
corroding the atmosphere

and yet
man will deny
his hand in her
downfall

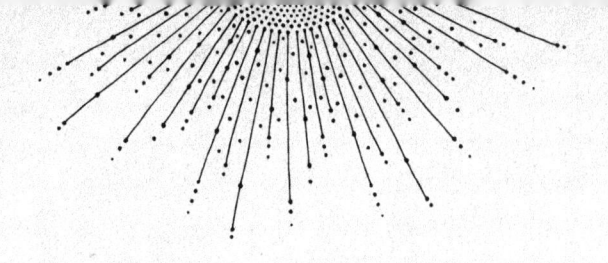

Proof

isn't the collective consciousness
scientifically proven?

all matter from one origin
the big bang
so wouldn't it make sense to say
we all belong to the same network?

fueled by the perpetual energy of
the big bang
the cosmos a reflection
of the neural connection linking us all

Shelter

here's the thing:
before you
I never faced myself

I ran
I hid
I started anew each time
pain crossed my path

but motherhood forces you
to sprout roots

and for each year of your life
I delve deeper into
Mother Earth

into myself

and I am forced to battle
the storms of my emotions
rather than take off
with the wind

so I can be a shelter for you
so one day
you can spread your wings
and fly

Sirens are Women for a Reason

leagues of our oceans have gone
unexplored

like these oceans
the depths of
femininity
have gone
unfathomed
by mankind

like the ocean
we look to the feminine
for calming and healing
but become repulsed
when they unleash
their power
their fury

to be so pivotal
in what sustains
mankind
and to be destroyed,
pilfered and poisoned
by the same
hand
injustices our oceans
and the feminine have both
suffered

the scales of universal order
have been tipped
by the heavy hand
of the patriarchy
for far too long

only upon respecting
our oceans
the feminine
and sacred Mother Earth
will balance be
restored

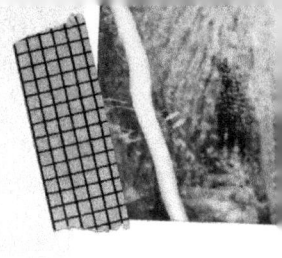

Spectrum of Faith

the human eye is only
capable
of perceiving
.0035% of the
electromagnetic spectrum

why were we born
into a world
allowed only a
minuscule
view of what was
created?

perhaps -
this existence
is meant
to reaffirm our faith

faith in our
internal compasses
and the
universal plan

what if
Lyra's compass
is a tool that resides
within us all

if only we could
tap into
our childlike
innocence
we could navigate
what is truly meant
for us

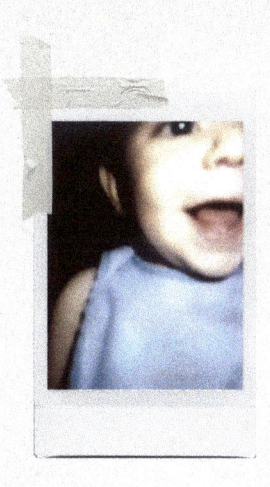

The Greatest Force on Earth

I am sick and tired
of being the
bigger person

immense fury
rises up in my chest
every time
I am forced
to send cordial words
to my oppressor

fury so deep
my chest is bound to
explode
wrenching the Earth in two

but
I contain the explosion

because the only force
greater than that
of a Mother's fury
is her
love

The Hierophant

he starts feigning love
he falsifies the reasoning
behind building walls around you
claiming protection
rather than capture

as his walls start to form
towering over you
you realize the sun is now absent
with the absence of
the warmth she provides
you become desperate
for any source of
heat

*"I see you peering over the walls,
inviting everyone and anyone to scale
them."
the heat of his
scorn
has you cowering
with outstretched arms*

a gaping wound
in your heart
still provides a
warm gush of blood

surely he is right
you must have committed
these heinous atrocities against him

walls don't just surround you
you are a wall
part of the architecture
to be broken down
and re-built at the hands of the architect

this goes on and on
until...

one day green graces your eyes
a leaf unfurling
breaking through
the stone of the courtyard
it is in this moment you remember
you resemble this graceful leaf
far greater than the unforgiving wall

you-yourself start to unfurl
slowly but surely
your sense of self
reawakens

the faux architect
wages storms against you
attempting to beat you down

your roots delve deep
into Mother Earth
and you remain
firm

you remember the sun
and her warmth
and anticipate soon
you will be in her presence again

still unfurling
now your branches
surpass the walls
roots degrading
them and their
imprisonment of you

you are vast

the faux architect
is a mere inkling
of the past

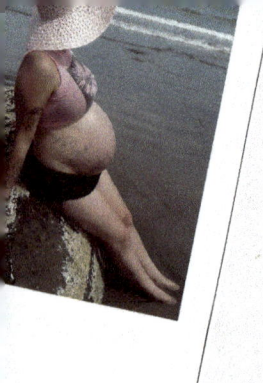

Transformation

when new human life
graces this planet

there is more than one
transformation
taking place

the birth of the
mother
and the death of the
maiden

it's easy to become caught
between two worlds
and lose yourself

until you find your footing
in this new role
and finally
emerge

you will be taken
aback by what
pours out of you

a ceaseless storm
of raw emotions
love
grief
happiness
guilt

once truly felt
acknowledged and expressed
the roots of your
new life can take hold
and you can grow into
who you are meant to be

no longer a
maiden
but a
mother

Transmuting

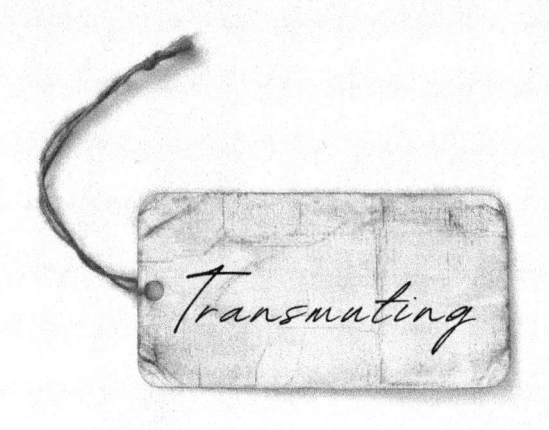

as they say
we were made
in the likeness of the
creator

and so we too are
creators

the ability to transform
pain into
beauty
runs through our veins

but how?

there is this illusion
that we simply
take pain and will it
away

but no
we are not alchemists
but artists

harnessing
pain
and using it
to fuel
our greatest
endeavors

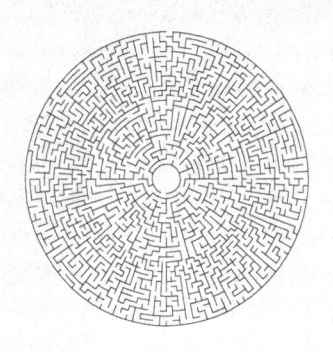

Trenches

in the midst of the
trenches
we lose perspective
lost in despair
plagued by the pain

but once we find ourselves
on the other side
perspective can grace us
again

perhaps
those trenches
were merely a maze
meant to lead us here

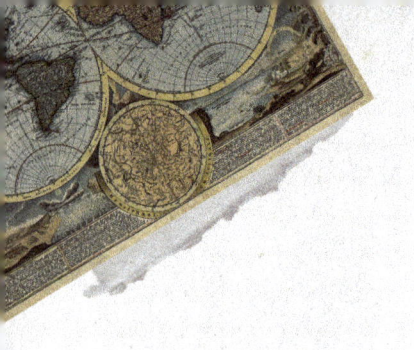

Two Worlds

I don't want to exist
me in my world
and you in yours

alongside one another

grazing here or there
never fully immersing
lacking depth and
understanding

I want to cohabitate
the same world
at the same time

your world only
consists of sunsets
and sunrises
a glory
assured to you daily

my world is turbulent
sometimes the sunrise is
eclipsed
by a hurricane

so you mistake my
S.O.S.
for a story

unable to grasp the
reality
of living in a world
that wasn't designed for
you

Voyage

parenthood is a
voyage at sea

your small boat
will be rocked
relentlessly
by the torrential
downpour that is
your child's emotions

when you embarked
on this adventure
you called yourself
captain

now humbled
and weathered
by the storm
you're a mere
passenger

the only tactic
that calms
the storm is
patience

so you float
along and
listen
to the
howling winds

no one told you
when you embarked
on this journey
that the sea would only
reflect
back to you
your own inner storms

and so
you surrender and
hope
your peace
will be reflected
back at you

What Broke My Heart

our nation's deepest
secret

once you become privy to the
truth
you are either
victim
or
perpetrator

a secret with such gargantuan
repercussions

the attack like
that of a nuclear
explosion
because growing
from such
destruction
is nearly
impossible

incest

molestation
a term more plausible
because it detaches the
responsibility
from the monsters
who live in your
home

molestation feels removed

some stranger snatching kids
when really
the demon lays next
to you at night

because according to the YWCA
93% of children know their abusers
and 96% of people who
abuse children are
male
and 76% are married men

why is it so
outlandish
when you scream the
truth
from the rooftops?

simple arithmetic will
corroborate

it is time to make a
stand

I used to be scared
to speak of this truth
publicly

but if the most innocent souls
on this planet
must live with the consequences
of the crimes committed against
them
then the monsters should too

The Aftermath

Chapter 2

Life is a vortex, yet somehow I now find myself at the eye of the storm. This vortex is one accepting and the conclusions I've made through allowing. Please, allow yourself as well. Do so and you too will find your way to the eye of the storm.

A Gift

today is the day I
decide
each time
love
walks into my life
I will welcome her
with open arms
instead of treating
her like an
intruder

I will give her a place
at my table and
laugh
play
cry
and discover

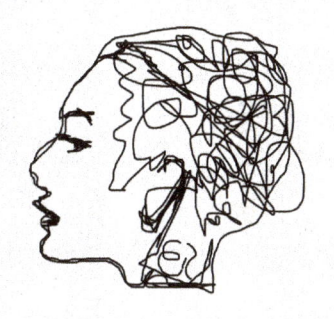

when and if
she excuses herself
I will thank her
for she was a
beacon
of light
illuminating the depths
of my own humanity

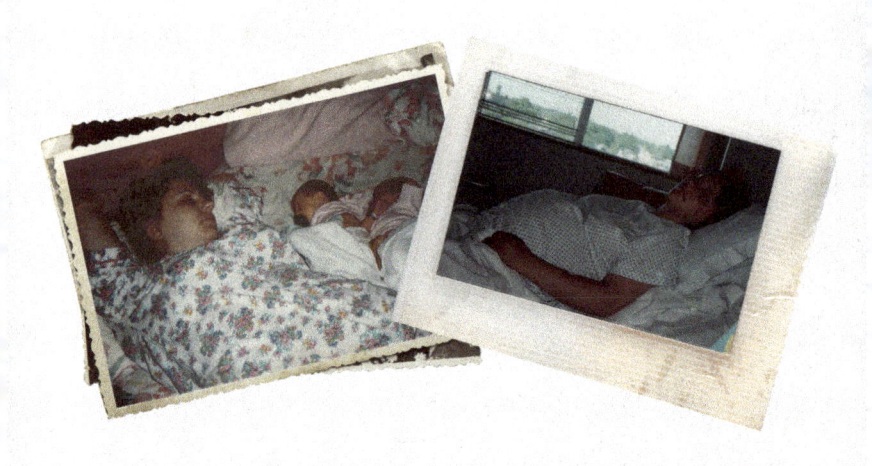

Born

you arrived on Earth
through a portal

imagine you hear
of another who
arrived
in the same manner

you would exclaim
proclaiming their power

and yet you
deny
your own

Carry On

motherhood has been difficult
not for the reasons you'd think
I am a chronic starter
the adrenaline of a new
project
goal
life purpose
mounting excitement
reaching its peak
then descending into disinterest

motherhood has taught me
there is more to an experience
than the initial euphoria
to appreciate life for its trials
to *know*
when you stick it out
trials are followed by
triumphs

Olivia Hamel

Dagger

in this reality of
uncertainties
the only surety
you will ever be
guaranteed
is your own inner truth

and the only people
who will ever benefit
from your silence
are your oppressors

so don't hand them
the dagger to slit
your own throat

Destination

I vividly remember
the sensation of
driving a car
for the first time

life is a bit like that

it can feel like
you're careening out of
control

but now I've learned
to embrace that feeling

because I am familiar
with this sensation
and I know
I'll arrive at my
destination

Destiny

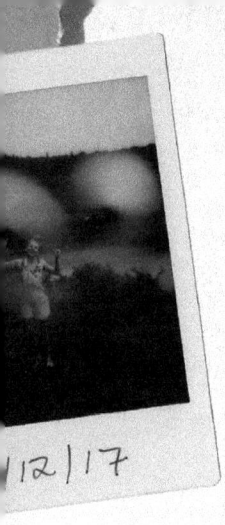

as I've grown older
I've found the tool
in the palm of my hand
is a compass
with only two directions

perform

or

express

the difference between
the two is clear

one drives you further
from
yourself

and the other brings you
straight
home

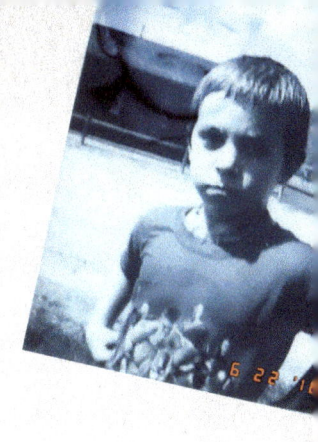

Ethereal

for a while I have had this fear
that if I wrote about anything
negative
even if it was something I had
experienced
and needed to express
that I would be attracting more
negativity to myself

when
in reality
it is what we keep
bottled inside of us
that contributes to our
magnetic field

we express our
negative feelings
and experiences
in order to set them
free

our frequencies
lighten

as does the load on our souls

flow

fear of loss
rejection and failure
is what impedes the
flow
of life

I've found
when I'm frightened
of losing something
I create a self-fulfilling
prophecy

but
when I picture
my desire
as something
to be cared for
nurtured and nestled

I then encourage
it from afar
only sending
love
and setting no
expectations
and from this
love
the flow of life returns
and the dream
blossoms

Foundation

remember when you
drove me home
in a snowstorm

we came to a hill
and started slipping
losing traction

fear struck me
flashbacks of car accidents
took hold of me

worried I asked
are we going to make it

you replied...
we might not make it
but we will be
okay

my nervous system
so wracked over the years
only knew one perspective
in times of "crisis"
I only knew
panic
now I know
true emergencies are rare
and so...

I am practicing this perspective
asking myself
if I don't
make it will I be
okay?

will I have a roof over my head?
will I have food to eat?
will I have water to bathe in?
will I have the support of my family?

these are the bricks
that make up the foundation
of my life

as long as this foundation survives
I will be
okay

Golden Hour

a moment I find myself
in with you

vibrant beauty
undulating around me

sunshine at my feet
and in the sky

your shining face
my own ray of sunshine

now
more than ever before
your innocence strikes me

in this moment
I remember
what it is like
to be at your stage
in the journey of life

how it feels to be in your
own bubble of reality

unbothered by
external forces

reveling in the beauty
around us

love
joy
playfulness
pungent in the atmosphere
striking as the cobalt sky
expanding above us

this moment seems infinite
but will forever be
cataloged as our
golden hour

Imagine

imagine
being born
with a compass
in the palm of your hand

but using a
crudely drawn
map instead

a catastrophe you allowed
every time you valued a man's
opinion above your own

this last time
was one too many

but rather than a dead end
you find yourself
in front of a
mirror

you glimpse your compass
and start the trek back home to
you

Lovers

in a pair of lovers
the sun and the moon
are always present

the sun casts her warmth
enveloping all around

the sun is inclusiveness personified

jovial
compassionate
encouraging

the sun
is steadfast

a surety
in a world fraught
with inconsistencies

some might take
the sun for granted

it's easy to overlook
a daily detail

but not the moon...

when she meets the sun
at dawn...
at dusk...

she is reminded
of stability

because with each meeting
she finds herself
varied

and although she embraces
life's cycles
and the necessity
for change

she revels in the
simple beauty
the sun brings to
their meetings

likewise
the sun
is reminded that her
enduring flame
is meant
to shine
in a way that casts the
shadows away

the sun and the moon
demonstrate to us
the importance
of a single meeting

how one instance
can start a cycle

I Love you
hope you have
a good day
beautiful
xoxo

Masterdoc

heteronormativity
was subtly poured into
my subconscious daily
yet there were some instances
that revealed to me
that the nails meant to
confine
me in that box
had not quite
sealed me in

and now...
light has perforated
those punctures
I am capable of seeing
what was always right
in front of
me

Olivia

when your namesake means
peace
it can be
challenging
to rise up against abuse
because women are
programmed to think
peace
is synonymous with
silence

what we
forget
is that
peace
is a result of
the waves of
justice rising up
and casting out
the "sinners"
(rapists, pedophiles, narcissists etc.)

the wave
our collective voices
and peace
not a bird perched on an arc
but the reassurance
of these voices
echoing against the water

Proximity

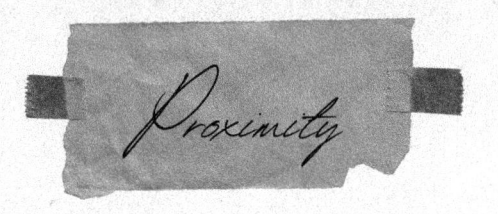

isn't it funny
how we tell others we are here
for them in their times of need
yet most times
all they need is for us to hear them

is it irony or fate
that the words are so
close
yet we often miss their
proximity

when we tell others
we are here we don't hear
we talk
we speak
we lament about
our own experiences

I am learning to be here to hear
to be a sounding board
for other's pain
because sometimes
that is all a broken heart requires to
heal

Purification

the beautiful thing
about fire is it
purifies

a perspective that will
only come later as a
revelation

because while you are
walking around burning alive
you aren't thinking about how forests
only stay healthy with the help of
wildfires

all that does not serve you
will burn away and fall to your feet

like the trees
you will take
the nutrients of
what has burned away

these are your lessons
and you grow stronger
reaching the canopy
closer to the sun
than ever before

Rooted

have you ever been
compelled
to criticize a tree

have you ever
gazed upon a tree
and found yourself
critiquing how her
bark is filled with
gouges gashes lines and lichen

so too
you will find
your beauty
is not marred
by your wrinkles
stretch marks
scars or acne
rather they reflect
the topography of
your natural beauty

Olivia Hamel

do you wrap
your arms
around her trunk
and wonder...
"If only she were smaller and I could
contain all of her within my arms?"

no
so why do you
condemn
yourself to shrink
into society's arms
a tight grip with
no room for love

do you scrutinize
each apple hanging
from her boughs
and fallen at her feet

each attempt you
have made at life
fallen or not
is just as beautiful

for you worked
ceaselessly
to produce
with the
courage and wisdom
to let go
when the time was
right

September

there is something about
swimming in september
on the precipice of autumn
one last glimpse of summer
on the edge of change
that must be why its called fall

in summer we are suspended
content and warm
in autumn we
fall
as the leaves do
back down to our roots

september is a time capsule
nostalgia refined down to its core
the air is thin like the pages of a book
chapters turn back as you dive into the
crisp water
for a brief moment you are ten again
as you break the surface
so too does the spell

Olivia Hamel

Settling

how about in the age of
aquarius
instead of settling
for less
we settle into
ourselves

sink
into our authenticity
and there
we will
bask

enveloped
in a blanket
of our highest
energy

Soul Mate

it is said
our guardian angels
love us from afar
rooting for us
waiting to intervene

all it takes
is a clear invitation
as they say
ask and you shall receive
and so...
I fell to my knees and
begged my angels
to bring my
soul mate
to me

but angels
never bring you
what you intend
but what you
need

and so laid
at my feet
was a gift
depicting to me
what love should
be

Sunflower

nature provides us with truth
time and time again

take the sunflower for example
always facing towards the
light
a clear metaphor for
optimism

but have you
ever asked yourself
where do they face
when life is devoid of light?

naturally they face
one another
so simple
that we pass this information over
when really
a profound lesson
is hidden within
waiting for humanity
to grasp onto it

like the sunflower
we too are innately drawn
towards warmth and light

in common society
we often find ourselves
lacking light

separated from one another
physically
mentally
spiritually
we suffer
society purposefully stacked in a way
to keep us disconnected
to maintain the status quo
at the expense of our souls

as the Age of Aquarius
dawns
humanity rises
although the
light is low
we know to
look to one another
to draw strength for what is to
come

The Great Debate

why is reincarnation
still up for debate?

when a flower
wilts
at the doorstep of
winter

and is revived
reborn
in spring

the soul
follows the
very same
cycle

the human body
can wither away
but the essence...
the *soul*
will always
flourish again

About the Author

She/her

My works are inspired by personal experience, with the hope that each word will be a guiding pinpoint of light in the dark night that is shadow work. My deepest desire is to aid in the inevitable awakening that is upon us. I have been lucky enough to be surrounded by loved ones who show me deep, unconditional love and support. Unfortunately, in this reality of existence, this type of bond is a rarity and a privilege. I vow to use my privilege to help all whom I am able to. Thank you for taking the time to read my book. If my words have sparked inspiration inside of you, please use that spark to ignite your own authentic and unique fire. You are light here to guide us out of the shadow age and into the Age of Aquarius.

About the Designer

Han (they/them) is a queer artist with their BFA. They have a deep love for art, social justice, animals, and family. Because of this, Han was happy to collaborate with Olivia on this project and bring to life some of these themes.

In their spare time, Han creates kaleidoscope-esque portraits to transform the old into the new. To view their work visit owleyereadings.com.

Connect with us

If you feel called to reach out to us please send an email to testortestament@gmail.com.

CPSIA information can be obtained
at www.ICGtesting.com
Printed in the USA
LVHW071707090822
725539LV00014B/387